teresa wilms montt

ANUARÍ

translated by
jessica sequeira

and with a prologue by
ramón del valle-inclán

THIS IS A SNUGGLY BOOK

ISBN: 978-1-64525-156-9

ANUARÍ

TERESA WILMS MONTT was born on September 8, 1893 in Viña del Mar, Chile. After the failure of her marriage in Santiago, her husband and family forced her to enter a convent, which she escaped with the help of Vicente Huidobro, to make a new life in Buenos Aires. Her first book, *Sentimental Doubts*, consisting of fifty poems with surrealist features, enjoyed great success in Argentine intellectual circles. In 1918, she moved to Madrid, where she published *In the Stillness of Marble* and *Anuarí*. She died in 1921, in Paris, from an overdose of Veronal.

JESSICA SEQUEIRA was born in San Jose, California. Her translations include Bernardo Couto Castillo's *Asphodels* (Snuggly Books, 2020), Enrique Gómez Carrillo's *Sentimental Stories* (Snuggly Books, 2019), Rafaela Contreras' *The Turquoise Ring and Other Stories* (Snuggly Books, 2019), and Adolfo Couve's *When I Think of My Missing Head* (Snuggly Books, 2018).

SNUGGLY BOOKS

Contents

Prologue / *7*

Anuarí / *13*

Translator's Note / *73*
Further Reading / *79*

Prologue

From what distant world does this strange voice reach us, bearing within it so many centuries and so much youth? It has the clear transparency of a song in the high peaks, and we do not know whether it is near to us or far away, when we hear it in the marvelous silence. As strange as this voice is the fragile blonde druidess who barely sets foot on earth, and walks with the rhythm of flight. Beneath the sacred mountain, she is made completely of snow and sun from the peaks. She sweeps along with her the esoteric prestige of some cult of wind and sea, earth and fire.

These poems, like the verses of a sacred book, rattle the chain of the centuries and have the mysterious resonance of elemental voices. A prophetic breath passes through them: The mud remembers the hour it emerged from chaos, as the spirit remembers the Divina Caligo. The grief of the fall is joined with the longing to return to the light. Splendid virtue of this voice that knocks at the bronze door of the Temple of Isis: Age-old echoes awaken and ancient shadows heed the incantation, guided by the music of her words that bloom like magic circles in the air of night.

This voice has an alexandrine grace. Within it, as in the den of an old alchemist, the green poisons of snakes and plants join with the crystalline stones on which Solomonic signs are graven, and with the bronze spheres that mark out the paths of stars, parallel to the paths of lives. Her marvelous alexandrine voice rekindles the shiver of apocalyptic visions and the mystical fever of the fakir, whose consciousness dissolves in the Great All.

—Valle-Inclán

ANUARÍ

Offering
To the blessed land
where my love rests.
Sweet Argentina!

I

You appeared, Anuarí, when I, with eyes blind and hands outstretched, was looking for you.

You appeared, and in my soul there was an explosion of life. All my inner flowers bloomed, and the bird of festive days sang.

You loved me, Anuarí, and I reached glory, suspended in your arms.

You disappeared, and I was left alone, my eyes shipwrecked in a night of tears.

Your shadow has grown kind, and between it and the grave, my soul waits for an hour.

II

I feel myself dying.

Alone in the wide bed with sheets of snow, I feel my poor feet returned from their pilgrimage to the heat losing themselves in the white steppe.

I have loved.

Twisted by passion, my arms wound like lewd snakes around the body of my master, and my lips full of kisses, like the sea with waves, dissolved like blood on his mouth.

Oh, warmth of affection! Like the sun in the fields, you stirred the flower of my breasts.

Pagan queen, queen of love, In musical torrents, I have given away the dazzling jewels of my young heart.

With a generous hand, without rushing the movements, I have lavished soft, harmonious caresses.

Anuarí!

Oh, dearest one! Oh, my love!

I spared nothing. But today I am poor and abandoned. My stiff feet suffer the pain of solitude and cold. My arms collapse over the cold amphoras of my hips, like snuffed-out altar candles at a funeral.

My feet have found warmth by pressing against each other like two little orphans.

I walk in oblivion, and slowly the stone slabs of my brain slide closed.

Anuarí, God and Beloved, look after me. I am going to sleep.

Amen!

III

My hands were light as two new doves. They floated down to earth to caress and remain ecstatic in idolatry, prostrate at the feet of a loved one.

Poor hands of mine! With their celestial whiteness they arrived to plead for kindness from chests where there was no heart.

They were soothing and gentle.

Poor hands of mine, how much cold you have suffered from such harsh lack of affection.

You were born beautiful to give beauty, and your warm palms became a nest for the adored head.

Hands of mine, you only know how to say goodbye with the strain of breaking rope.

Hands of mine! Faint with sorrow, you have also wrapped the adored body in a winding sheet.

IV

The winds shriek, beating against doors and windows, tearing down trees, churning up rivers.

Jackals and panthers roam with eyes blinded by sand, backs bristling.

Dull noises from erupting volcanos, from swelling seas, join the howl of the cyclone.

In cemeteries the shudder of corpses is heard, the hollow gnashing of teeth in an empty skull.

Cold as a stab into rock, a human cry comes from the distance. Help!

V

Anuarí, I loved you.

For my soul there was no music like that of your teeth chattering from lust.

They were polished stones that fell from the moon into the open wound of your lips.

I kissed the purple of your mouth and shuddered with pleasure in the symphony of the supreme sigh, that sigh of plenitude which travels like a spirit toward the eternal.

Anuarí, I loved you so much that I now exalt the stars with lyricism.

VI

In the twilight, the windowpane returns me the mirror image of my face.

I curl my mouth into a smile, and see my skull through the transparent flesh.

My hair stuck to my temples limply falls, like a curtain of golden ash.

In the depths of my eyes my thoughts press into me with piercing black tips, digging holes of new depth into my skull.

Shadow, silence, nothing exists to satisfy the restlessness of my vital lamp.

My spirit, forever wandering and eternal, lives in its world of dream, invoking its sister death.

VII

The transparent grape hung from the vine.

Like the fox of legend, my watering lips waited, open slightly, lusting for the fruit.

At my feet the amphora offered itself, brimming with fragrant, refreshing wine, and my instinct was there below with it.

I bit into the fruit, I felt the glory of dawn in my throat; I drank the wine, and the warm invigorating blood of the earth darkened my brow, measured my heartbeats.

I felt young partaking of the grape, wise and old partaking of wine.

VIII

I walked through a cemetery passage.

Amidst the gray tombstones and gloomy ivy, all at once a note of light and heat caressed my eyes.

It was a tea rose.

I came up to her and spoke with that language only we lovers of blue possess, the language that one speaks to flowers and precious stones, and asked her:

"Where do you come from, Princess Tea?"

The embalmed rose opened her petals toward the Necropolis, and with a voice of foliage and fountain, she answered:

"My cradle was a young skull. My petals are the hours of love from a maiden who forgot to wake when she was fifteen years old.

"She sleeps still, and over her bed I sing the song of her kisses to nightingales and larks.

"When evening comes, the nightingale refreshes his lyrical throat with the first pearl of moisture given to me by the dew, and when it grows light, the lark comes to look for the gentleness in my heart it needs to awaken the beings of the living world."

The cawing of a crow silenced the voice of the rose, which tucked itself away into its petals, shy and childish.

I kneeled down then on the stone, and with that language spoken to flowers, said goodbye to the dead maiden.

"Sleep, juvenilia, dreaming of the love that ignited your soul.

The earth is a beloved being, with narcotic lips and flesh of petal."

IX

The night gifted a star to the marsh.

At the center of the muddy sphere, the heavenly body irradiated within the green putrefaction, that palace of reptiles.

And in chorus around them, from the lotus of poison, toads emerged to disturb the calm of the valleys with their sinister croaks.

The eagle woke, and abandoning the rock, soared toward the flatlands.

The shining point revealed its pride.

It believed that it was tearing through the blue to brush a star, and plunged into the foul marsh.

The bird of prey carried away the star into the depths, imprinted on its majestic wings.

Gasping like worn-out instruments, the reptiles and the toads burst, their bodies destroyed.

X

She departed like wine.

Sheathed to her eyes in gray cloth.

She was by my side for a minute, a century.

Her forehead shone like polished marble, and I glimpsed an ironic grimace beneath the covering.

She said nothing.

She departed like wine, but left escorted by a long line of black ants.

Her face shone like an altar candle, and I glimpsed a stabbing pain beneath the covering.

XI

I love the Nothing, for the Nothing is the All,
and the All is myself when I think and love.

XII

I was alone, it was night.

I waited for the hands that would come to piously dress her body in dark cloth.

The yellow feet were as rigid as two pieces of wood laid out for a cross.

Waxen light came in through the glass, and I glimpsed a sky with a waning moon.

I approached the dead woman. She was decapitated.

I ran the rag over her severed neck and left slowly.

I stopped, frozen stiff.

A whirlwind of long black locks swayed from her chopped-off head.

Looking at her, I thought she was coming back to me, and her two ecstatic eyes terrified me, full of a poisonous liquid from beneath the earth that stained the shadows with the perverse brightness of Prussian blue.

XIII

The cat is asleep, curled up on the armchair.

Like water from dead pearls, evening light trickles through my window.

On my table, spread out, the deck of cards awaits the prophesy.

On the wall a portrait hanging upside-down bleeds shadows from its mouth.

With arms crossed at the base of my neck, I look without seeing.

I wait . . .

XIV

One night in darkness, I sat in front of the mirror.

The gaze of all things weighed on my back, the ecstatic gaze of time.

Like the passage of the moon over sleeping waters, all at once the mirror filled with light, and in its unfathomable depth I saw the dead body of Anuarí.

A gigantic lotus emerged from the shroud, the hand on his heart, as long as the shadow on the wall.

Anuarí, my beloved.

Why has your left hand grown so much?

"Oh, woman I loved! For my spirit to live in the realms of mystery, it needs to nourish itself with souls that inhabit mortal bodies. And this hand of mine grows larger from scavenging, from stealing the best of the hearts that have loved me in life."

Anuarí. I love you, take my life.

"You grow paler day by day, woman I loved, and the dark circles are two ebony frames for the blue of your eyes. My hand is made of velvet, you never felt when I stole from you. You offered me the casket without realizing that my magnet absorbed your jewel."

Anuarí, Anuarí, I screamed in strangled anguish.

The mirror faded, and I felt the things around me take on a glacial calm.

Something abrupt pierced my skeleton.

My days are numbered.

In the solitude of my thoughts, I hear a grave being dug.

XV

The cup trembled in my hands, making the green opal poison flash with the colors of the whole spectrum.

In a frenetic dance, my eyes shifted from their orbits.

I brought the glass to my lips, and the magnet of absinthe absorbed my pupils.

From the depths they looked at me, mocking, elongated with pleasure.

I drank the liquid, and squeezed those eyes with a single bite, as if they were the fruit of the snake.

XVI

Decapitated, she with the mutilated arms, entirely white, the host of art, gives the peace of the temple to this disordered study.

Artificial light bathes her body with respectful tremors, traveling with shivers of admiration from the amphora of her hips to her bold breasts.

Venus de Milo had no heart, and was the soul of genius.

I left the reddest of my carnations on the plinth, the one that stained the blood of my pleasure and my pain.

The beauty of the centuries seemed even paler now, bled white, as if she had rolled toward the bottoms of her feet that throbbing heart of hers which inspires eternal devotions.

XVII

He comes every night to my bedroom. Without eyes he looks at me, without a mouth he speaks to me, and the deep silence of his gaze and voice are those of the buried.

He is very far away and he is with me, he thinks with my brain and cries with my tears.

When I behave badly, Anuarí punishes my bones, piercing into them with the ice pick of a toothless laugh.

XVIII

She has made her fingers into magic flutes. Since she has no flesh, the sounds travel freely up through her hollow arms.

At night she comes to give a serenade to those in the asylum. She curls up under a tree and blows on the little finger which produces music all four seasons of the year.

A desire for mockery shakes her entire body, and with a nervous laugh like someone being tickled, she blows on all her fingers.

And the world begins its frenetic dance without rest, casting out fire through its luminous orbit.

The epileptic seas vomit iridescent foam along the coasts, and the cataclysmic laugh of the mountains tumbles forth like a roar, and makes it spit out all its teeth.

The moon has hurt the corner of its lips, and drips its mother-of-pearl blood over the globe.

Nothing can stop the catastrophic serenade.

The poor ones in the asylum without muscles and without entrails do ridiculous dances, with the rhythm of sails in the wind, until their jutting hips slacken.

And she, taken over by madness, blows and blows on her fingers without realizing that her skeleton has grown burning red as hot coals.

She is the Empress.

Slowly she opens a marble door, and behind her appears the latest one in the asylum, who was admitted during the day.

With eyes full of sleep, still under the influence of the black narcotic, she comes down from her niche and approaches the madwoman with an expression of love.

Her body is young and beautiful.

She stops her whistling, startled by the apparition.

Everything returns to its place, and life is extinguished.

Feline, jealous, pale with lust, she buries her polished skull into the young chest and bursts into sobs.

With a shudder, the mirror of dawn splits in two.

XIX

Follow me, said Anuarí.

His blue eyes transparent with light, fixed onto mine, pierced through the veils of my primitive darkness.

And I followed him.

He led me by the hand to the path where the sun appears, where the soul of the world takes shelter at night, and with his marble finger pointed toward the abyss full of flowers.

For the first time, I felt the breath that came from my chest blend together with the blue.

XX

A strange gust plunged me to Earth.

I do not know why I am here!

When will he take me?

He left behind the mute astonishment of my eyes upon all things, the sadness of some words not understood.

When will he take me?

Deep nostalgia fills me for that world where I have never been.

When will he come for me!

XXI

With hands open, the palms flat like a snowy little stage where nymphs might dance, I have arranged myself to offer you the sole truths of the wise or blessed.

One palm is a diamond with a thousand facets, the other is a hard colorful stone, cracked like the face of a miser.

I offer you, upon these clean palms, severe as the figures of an Egyptian relief, my love for myself and my egoism.

Anuarí, spirit.

Do not smile at me like a man.

XXII

The Sly Lady is very cunning.

She frightens children and men with her waxen face.

The sound of her bones is a rattle that gives greater merriment to the starving Harlequins that dance grotesquely, finding no end to the roads.

When the Sly One laughs, the owls in the cypresses faint with hysterical convulsions, and the tubercular maiden of the heavens covers herself, terrified, with the blanket of clouds.

The Sly Lady has no essence, but is phosphorescent.

XXIII

Beati qui lugent quoniam et ipsi consolabuntur.[†]

Yes. Admirable prophet, I will weep over the steps of your temple.

I will leave them polished so that your feet covered in sores might come to them and be refreshed.

Nazarene, in the golden light of a votive candle, your hair will be my shroud.

I will cry until I feel your hand come and offer itself as a soft bed to my heart.

Jesus, then I no longer will see the stars, because I will carry them within my eyes.

You were beloved by my soul, Anuarí!

---

† From the Gospel of Matthew 5:5, "Blessed are those who mourn, for they shall be comforted."

XXIV

The Bengal tiger howls and roars in his cage.

His claws slam against the bars with sounds of steel.

We humans think the owner of the jungles is in heat.

The tiger is king, and is nostalgic for the blue and the stars, because the fierce beast of Bengal has breathed the air of the fakirs, with its centuries and wisdom.

The magnificent beast wears a coat of gold sky and black comets.

XXV

Power of the signs traced by the hand, mysterious kabbalah.

It is the fifth letter of the Abracadabra, it is in the Cosmos.

In it begins the fatal augury of the first sin.

Upon naming it, good hands make the sign of the cross, and others touch iron.

When a voice pronounces it, the dark Egyptian woman on the road shouts the enormous sacred blasphemies.†

† The fifth letter of the Hebrew alphabet is *hei*, which symbolizes both repentance and a return to one's essential self. The Egyptian might be a reference to Saint Mary of Egypt, who retired to the desert after a life of prostitution.

But I love it, and it is my talisman in solitude and shadow.

When there is no shelter for the two of us in the world, in my heart I give love to its skin of stone.

Carried by the winds, our eyes traveling to the stars, we lose ourselves in the sea of the world, our throats gorged as a siren's whistle.

XXVI

Dressed in a black mantle, he came last night through the mirror.

His hands crossed over his chest emerged from the black sleeve like lily petals.

The abyss of his eyes swallowed all the shadows, and in my brain became light.

His mouth spoke without words, like the old organs of the cathedrals, and said: Sleep, sleep, for dream is the dawn of eternal day.

XVII

In the mornings, the song of the trees is fresh and clear like the voice of a child.

And at noon, it becomes warm beneath the sun, remembering the dialogues of lovers.

The tree imitates the confidential notes of the sad older folk at dusk, and at night resurrects the gentleness of their song.

The trees are men of the earth. When they bend over, they are thinking, and when they raise their branches, it is to embrace the infinite.

The trees are godly men.

XVIII

Through the stem of a headless flower, Anuarí appeared last night.

The water in the vase boiled, and the petals of the other flowers fell away.

With his paradisiacal slowness, Anuarí touched my eyes, giving me the torpor of death.

With a single pang, my heart started up.

My anesthetized body was left behind amidst the august calm of statues.

Opal light murkily surrounded his figure, and the objects.

I saw how Anuarí came, lifting the red stain of my heart to his mouth, and heard the dripping of hot blood imitate the passage of hours in the subterranean silence.

XIX

A woman with bronze skin and a lustful mouth brushed against me, in passing.

Her walk brought to mind a snake.

I looked at her eyes, and in the discs of her pupils, first luminous, then opaque, the centuries slid by.

At my curious and terrified insistence, the woman smiled.

Her smile was polished mother-of-pearl from the inner stone of a pyramid.

Cleopatra! I whispered to her, and the unknown one fled, undulating and enigmatic as a snake.

XXX

Last night he came to me, passing through the closed door like moonlight.

He moved the draperies and chiffons from his path with a trembling of breeze.

Putting put a finger on my forehead, he drew out all thought.

I saw my ideas float like a burning liquid through his body of mist; I saw how upon arriving at his heart, the intensity of a memory shook everything within him.

I saw his intangible covering darken when in the conjectures of my thoughts, the first lie swept past.

And I heard the cry, like a beating of wings, that he placed upon my lips as he left through the closed door, from a heart as tender as moonlight.

XXXI

In the vault of my skull echoes the voice of silence, the voice of the centuries that cross the human abysses.

Through my mouth speak Buddha, Christ, Mohammed.

My heart learnedly receives the old maxims of luminous apostles.

That chaotic voice of silence penetrates my body's covering with spirals of snow.

Speak to me, voice of the dead, and I will offer myself to the constellations.

XXXII

I have breathed in the fragrance of a red car-
nation, and stabbing memories gave fire to my
pupils.

My heart, like a handful of mercury, slid
along my body until coming to rest at my feet.

XXXIII

I stood at the balcony to search the skies for the illusion and withdraw afterward to my wide bed, my solitude forgotten.

A dazzling star passed by, fleeting.

Safe travels, sister detached from your world, celestial wanderer of the cosmic soul.

Safe travels, sister, now we will join the Nothingness when Anuarí orders the conjunction of stars and men.

I slept on my back in the bed.

The archaic figure of funeral calm, a shadow of the magician fakir that preceeded Christ, stopped inside my window frame. He smiled at me with the wisdom of the cold, hieratic Cosmos.

He kept moving. His long beard unfurled with the rhythm of his swelling cape, a sail in the cutting black wind that hides the light of the stars.

On my table the pages of *The Marvelous Lamp* by D. Ramón María del Valle-Inclán stretched their arms toward me from the shadow.

XXXIV

When I opened my door, I felt strike my senses the breath of another life, which must dwell somewhere nearby.

I looked at the sky outside, I observed the portraits, I checked the mirror.

Then through the windowpanes I saw a white cloud pass by, and I understood.

In chaste praise, my heart became a fleur de lis and broke at the feet of my idol, Anuarí.

XXXV

Facing my closed window, I ask time how much longer I must live.

Shadows flood my blinds, and the light barely marks out a slender line.

The clock has the hesitations of a sick heart.

With a convulsive gesture, my hands twitch on the page.

They look for the support of the earth.

XXXVI

Cautiously, with hermetic steps, she went underground.

There she folded her veils of an Indian dancer; there she sunk her head into her arms, released her perfumed hair over the slabs, and dreamed.

The stars cry because they cannot come down to the cave, the stars believe that their queen suffers and uneasily wink their eyes.

XXXVII

Kneeling, arms crossed, my face turned toward the sky, I await the miracle.

My eyelids close, and a wing suspends my body.

I fly, I dream.

My brain throbs in the ether devoid of the box of a skull, receiving Saturn's gaze on its naked mass, that red gaze which is fulminating, creative.

Without the power to reach me, the snake stretches out its head, swaying the fine wire of its body, electric with envy.

The miracle took place at daybreak.

XXXVIII

Eyes closed, I try to fall asleep.

In waves of strange colors, the night descends toward my pupils, marking the shapes of ghosts distant in my memory.

With the steps of a hero, my thought marches on, digging its heels into the back of my neck, brusquely doing turns like a grinding mill.

On the night table, purple hyacinths exhale their poisonous breath, filling my lungs with sweet, bitter heaviness.

There is a solitude in my being like that of a leaf drowned in the pond.

Seeking light in the heart of the constellations, Anuarí abandoned me.

Pensive, with the rigor of granite, I lean into myself and sink into the chaos of my Nothingness.

XXXIX

She ordered it done.

The chimera of the Infinite has ceased.

The column of the centuries has stopped transforming into opaque stones, and the world has ended in chaos with the crackle of burning charcoal.

XL

The turquoise of my ring was blue like my eyes.
    I loved, I suffered, I meditated.
    The turquoise of my ring has turned green,
and has the severity of an emperor who judges.

XLI

If she comes for me, tell her I am not here.

And if despite your refusal, she enters, tell her I will go meet her where the Two Paths cross.

Bring her to my room, and show her a little black toy under the pillow, which men invented to call her.

Tell her I went to look for flowers, because I like their silken coverings.

XLII

Twilight, dream of day.

My face leans its pain of life into your fragile, dying arms.

Twilight. Gold of dawn, violet of death, the mystical poison wrapped in your half tints descends toward men.

The illuminated ones stroke images in your shadow, the sad ones know how to adore their pain, and those who have never loved weep for a love.

Magician twilight, at once boy and old man, you light your lamp under the water of the lakes, melancholy pastor of foreboding.

XLIII

My laugh drowned in the mirror.

The silver glass sent a long, sinister crackling into the night.

One, two . . . the hour was silent, the cold metal of a planet within a rigid swamp.

Epileptic with arousal, the moon surrendered itself to the balconies.

And the corpse of my laugh becomes a delicate emerald that upon dissolving, sends rings and shining crosses up to the surface.

XLIV

He is going, I feel it in the cold of my blood!

He is going, and nothing will be able to stop him, because he is eternal and would pass through my arms.

And I cannot kill my body, because then my soul would take another path opposed to his, and the separation would be eternal.

Anuarí is going, and I feel the vertigo of an angel falling from the blue abyss into the flames of the infernal cave.

XLV

My head is the great fountain that chose the reflections of boreal tones.

And my body curved in the air is like a religious pavilion, a white platform for the eternal light.

My eyes are human reservoirs in which the stars affectionately submerge themselves, seeking the passionate caress of the earth.

And my soul, a dead star that blindly spins for eternity, consuming itself in the destructive fire that purifies and generates.

Oh, life! what a small circle you have given me, where the entirety of my creative force cannot be unleashed.

FIN

Anuarí! Anuarí!

Profound spirit, return from the chaos.

Come back in a mysterious covering, guest of my glacial nights.

May your fingers of dream rest upon my sleepless eyelids.

Close them, Anuarí.

Sublime poison, give death to my terrified brain.

Linger over my grave, with an enigmatic smile.

Smiles from the afterlife, of shadow and light, tremendous smile that annihilates me.

Profound spirit, return from the chaos!

All of my flowers have died, and to sate your hunger there remains only the bleeding wound of my broken heart.

Anuarí, Anuarí, I succumb to the whirlwind of the mad stars tumbling past!

Return from the chaos!

Translator's Note

Anuarí (Madrid, 1918) has much in common with the Chilean poet's previous works *Inquietudes sentimentales* (Buenos Aires, 1917, translated as *Sentimental Doubts*) and *En la quietud del mármol* (Madrid, 1918, translated as *In the Stillness of Marble*). The anthology *Lo que no se ha dicho* (1922) even confused these texts. In *Anuarí*, however, there is a greater emphasis on sound and music, which for Wilms Montt have mystical qualities that not only express emotion, but also have the power to influence the outside world, according to the beliefs of esoteric philosophy. In *Anuarí*, almost all the poems mention sounds emitted by human bodies, animals or instruments, which can result in pleasure, madness, magic, destruction or creation.

The author's emotional responses often interact with these sounds, suggesting a fertile relationship between the inner life and the external sensory world that goes beyond personal experience. Wilms Montt's fascination with music seems to be partly an influence of Valle-Inclán's work; she mentions *La lámpara maravillosa* explicitly in *Anuarí* ("On my table the pages of *The Marvelous Lamp* by D. Ramón María del Valle-Inclán stretched their arms toward me from the shadow"), and Valle-Inclán himself wrote the introduction to *Anuarí*, emphasizing its musical qualities in an extensive metaphor about words, voices, resonances, echoes, rhythms and silences in the work. For both Wilms Montt and Valle-Inclán, sound and music are linked to the world beyond this one, and to the elevation of the spirit. Silence is also present, in many ways: the reverberations of what is left unstated.

It is often said of Wilms Montt that her biography is inseparable from her work, and she is read as a melodramatic and mythical figure in Chilean literature, as she supposedly fled from Santiago to Buenos Aires to escape a loveless marriage and convent life, and wrote her books of poems about an unrequited lover Horacio Ramos Mejía, who killed himself in front of her. He, in a reversal of traditional gender roles, is thus considered a kind of muse for her. But this biographical narrative of the rebellious poet and the libertarian femme fatale, in a dense atmosphere of eroticism and tragedy, perhaps occludes other readings of her work and her poetic use of sensory description.

In *Anuarí*, although the premise of the death of the loved one is still present, the images are new (a beheading, animal choirs, a carnival dance), and the musical emphasis creates space for another way of understanding Wilms Montt's writing, emphasizing the importance of sound and music in spiritual life. Along with other writers and artists of her time, Wilms Montt considered emotion and music to be capable of affecting reality itself—an idea also found in mystic philosophy and religions of Asia—such that emotion is not only a personal response to events, but something possible to develop along with others through disciplined techniques and processes of self-training, in a practical education of the senses. *Anuarí* was published in 1918 by the Madrid publisher Martínez de Velasco, and signed with the name Teresa de la ✝; it is dedicated to Argentina, where along with tango, Wilms Montt developed a taste for the works of the Indian poet Rabindranath Tagore, whom she read along with friends she made there. The Chilean poet Vicente Huidobro had helped Wilms Montt to cross the cordillera, escaping the convent "La Preciosa Sangre" she was forced by her family to enter after the tumultuous end of her marriage with the aristocrat Gustavo Balmaceda Valdés, leaving behind two small daughters. Until the melodramatic suicide of Mejía—the jilted Argentine lover—the years in Buenos Aires seem to have been relatively happy ones. After this traumatic event, Wilms Montt moved to New York to work as a nurse for the Red Cross, but was forced to leave after being accused of being a German spy. She then continued on to Madrid, where she lived for a couple of years before taking her own life at the age of twenty-eight.

In the present book, Wilms Montt enters into dialogue with Anuarí, without quotation markings. (I added a few in the translation, for clarity.) As she puts herself into the consciousness of the dead man, the confusion of voices and bodies makes it seem as if the poet were not only mourning a beloved, but also entering his consciousness, putting words in his mouth for her, making his desire for death her own. The poet, the decapitated Venus de Milo, the tea rose, the dead young woman, the Sly Lady and the spirit of Anuarí become reflected versions, moving fluidly between bodies and voices. Beyond these oneiric scenes of conversation with those beyond the grave, with their mirror play and changes of perspective, Wilms Montt also resurrects some kind of meaning for macabre events through her song. Reading her words with attention, the esoteric power of her poems passes to us, the readers. In our own minds and time, we bring her spirits back to life.

—Jessica Sequeira

Further Reading

Del Valle-Inclán, Ramon. *La lámpara maravillosa. Ejercicios espirituales*. Madrid: SGEL, Imp. Artes de la Ilustración, 1922.

González-Vergara, Ruth. *Teresa Wilms Montt: un canto de libertad*. Santiago de Chile: Grijalbo, 1993.

Subercaseaux, Bernardo. *Historia de las ideas y de la cultura en Chile*. Santiago: Editorial Universitaria, 1997.

Wilms Montt, Teresa. *Anuarí*. Madrid: Casa Ed. Blanco, 1918.

Wilms Montt, Teresa. *Anuarí*. Madrid: Editorial Torremozas, 2017.

Wilms Montt, Teresa. *Poesía reunida*. Santiago: Editorial Alquimia, 2016.

Wilms Montt, Teresa. *Obras completas*. Sevilla: Editorial Renacimiento, 2023.

A PARTIAL LIST OF SNUGGLY BOOKS

ETHEL ARCHER *The Hieroglyph*
ETHEL ARCHER *Phantasy and Other Poems*
ETHEL ARCHER *The Whirlpool*
G. ALBERT AURIER *Elsewhere and Other Stories*
CHARLES BARBARA *My Lunatic Asylum*
CHARLES BARBARA *Stirring Stories*
JULES-AMÉDÉE BARBEY D'AUREVILLY *Hannibal's Ring*
NATALIE CLIFFORD BARNEY *The One Who is Legion*
S. HENRY BERTHOUD *Misanthropic Tales*
MAY ARMAND BLANC *The Last Rendezvous*
LÉON BLOY *The Tarantulas' Parlor and Other Unkind Tales*
PETRUS BOREL *The Treasure of the Arcueil Cavern*
ÉLÉMIR BOURGES *The Twilight of the Gods*
ADA BUISSON *The Baron's Coffin*
CYRIEL BUYSSE *The Aunts*
KAREL ČAPEK *Krakatit*
BERNARDO COUTO CASTILLO *Asphodels*
JAMES CHAMPAGNE *Harlem Smoke*
FÉLICIEN CHAMPSAUR
    The Emerald Princess and Other Decadent Fantasies
FÉLICIEN CHAMPSAUR *The Latin Orgy*
ARMAND CHARPENTIER *Claustrophobic Madness*
BRENDAN CONNELL *Unofficial History of Pi Wei*
BRENDAN CONNELL (editor) *The Zaffre Book of Occult Fiction*
BRENDAN CONNELL (editor)
    The Zinzolin Book of Occult Fiction
RAFAELA CONTRERAS *The Turquoise Ring and Other Stories*
DANIEL CORRICK (editor)
    Ghosts and Robbers: An Anthology of German Gothic Fiction
ADOLFO COUVE *When I Think of My Missing Head*
RENÉ CREVEL *Are You All Crazy?*
QUENTIN S. CRISP *Aiaigasa*
QUENTIN S. CRISP *Graves*
LUCIE DELARUE-MARDRUS *Amanit*
LUCIE DELARUE-MARDRUS *The Last Siren and Other Stories*
LADY DILKE *The Outcast Spirit and Other Stories*

CATHERINE DOUSTEYSSIER-KHOZE
   The Beauty of the Death Cap
ÉDOUARD DUJARDIN *Hauntings*
BERIT ELLINGSEN *Now We Can See the Moon*
ERCKMANN-CHATRIAN *A Malediction*
ALPHONSE ESQUIROS *The Enchanted Castle*
ZDRAVKA EVTIMOVA *Laura and Other Stories*
ENRIQUE GÓMEZ CARRILLO *Sentimental Stories*
DELPHI FABRICE *Flowers of Ether*
DELPHI FABRICE *The Red Sorcerer*
DELPHI FABRICE *The Red Spider*
BENJAMIN GASTINEAU *The Reign of Satan*
GUSTAVE GEFFROY *Decadent Tapestries*
EDMOND AND JULES DE GONCOURT *Manette Salomon*
REMY DE GOURMONT *From a Faraway Land*
REMY DE GOURMONT *Morose Vignettes*
GUIDO GOZZANO *Alcina and Other Stories*
LUIGI GUALDO *Narcisa and Other Stories*
GUSTAVE GUICHES *The Modesty of Sodom*
ALTHEA GYLES *A Woman Without a Soul and Other Writings*
EDWARD HERON-ALLEN *The Complete Shorter Fiction*
EDWARD HERON-ALLEN *Three Ghost-Written Novels*
RHYS HUGHES *Cloud Farming in Wales*
J.-K. HUYSMANS *The Crowds of Lourdes*
J.-K. HUYSMANS *Knapsacks*
COLIN INSOLE *Valerie and Other Stories*
JUSTIN ISIS *Pleasant Tales II*
JULES JANIN *The Dead Donkey and the Guillotined Woman*
LIONEL JOHNSON *The Complete Winchester Letters*
VICTOR JOLY
   The Unknown Collaborator and Other Legendary Tales
GUSTAVE KAHN *The Mad King*
KLABUND *Spook*
MARIE KRYSINSKA *The Path of Amour*
BERNARD LAZARE *The Gate of Ivory*
BERNARD LAZARE *The Mirror of Legends*
BERNARD LAZARE *The Torch-Bearers*
JULES LERMINA *Human Life*

MAURICE LEVEL *The Shadow*
JEAN LORRAIN *Errant Vice*
JEAN LORRAIN *Fards and Poisons*
JEAN LORRAIN *Masks in the Tapestry*
JEAN LORRAIN *Monsieur de Bougrelon and Other Stories*
JEAN LORRAIN *Nightmares of an Ether Drinker*
JEAN LORRAIN *Princesses of Darkness and Other Exotica*
JEAN LORRAIN *The Soul Drinker and Other Decadent Fantasies*
JEAN LORRAIN *The Turkish Lady and Other Writings*
GEORGES DE LYS *An Idyll in Sodom*
GEORGES DE LYS *Penthesilea*
ARTHUR MACHEN *N*
ARTHUR MACHEN *Ornaments in Jade*
PAUL MARGUERITTE *Pantomimes and Other Surreal Tales*
HENRI MARTIN *Isuren*
CAMILLE MAUCLAIR *The Frail Soul and Other Stories*
CATULLE MENDÈS *Bluebirds*
CATULLE MENDÈS *For Reading in the Bath*
CATULLE MENDÈS *Mephistophela*
OSCAR MÉTÉNIER *Three Decadent Stories*
ÉPHRAÏM MIKHAËL *Halyartes and Other Poems in Prose*
LUIS DE MIRANDA *Paridaiza*
LUIS DE MIRANDA *Who Killed the Poet?*
OCTAVE MIRBEAU *The 628-E8*
OCTAVE MIRBEAU *The Death of Balzac*
GAURAV MONGA *Costumes of the Living*
RICHARD O'MONROY *The Last Waltz and Other Stories*
CHARLES MORICE *Babels, Balloons and Innocent Eyes*
MANUEL MAGALLANES MOURE *What is Love*
MONTESQUIEU *The Temple of Gnide*
GABRIEL MOUREY *Monada*
DAMIAN MURPHY *The Acephalic Imperial*
DAMIAN MURPHY *Daughters of Apostasy*
DAMIAN MURPHY *The Exalted and the Abased*
DAMIAN MURPHY *The Star of Gnosia*
KRISTINE ONG MUSLIM *Butterfly Dream*
OSSIT *Ilse*
PHILOTHÉE O'NEDDY *The Enchanted Ring*

CHARLES NODIER *Jean Sbogar and Other Stories*
CHARLES NODIER *The Memoirs of Maxime Odin*
CHARLES NODIER *Outlaws and Sorrows*
CHARLES NODIER
   The Story of the King of Bohemia and his Seven Castles
HERSH DOVID NOMBERG *A Cheerful Soul and Other Stories*
HERSH DOVID NOMBERG *Happiness and Other Fiction*
EDITH OLIVIER *Horror! Horror! Horror!*
GEORGES DE PEYREBRUNE *A Decadent Woman*
HÉLÈNE PICARD *Sabbat*
URSULA PFLUG *Down From*
JEAN PRINTEMPS *Whimsical Tales*
RACHILDE *The Demon of the Absurd*
RACHILDE *The Blood-Guzzler and Other Stories*
RACHILDE *The Princess of Darkness*
JEREMY REED *Bad Boys*
JEREMY REED *Surrender to a Stranger*
JEREMY REED *When a Girl Loves a Girl*
ADOLPHE RETTÉ *Misty Thule*
JEAN RICHEPIN *The Bull-Man and the Grasshopper*
FREDERICK ROLFE (Baron Corvo) *Amico di Sandro*
FREDERICK ROLFE (Baron Corvo)
   An Ossuary of the North Lagoon and Other Stories
JASON ROLFE *An Archive of Human Nonsense*
ARNAUD RYKNER *The Last Train*
WILLIAM SEABROOK
   Astounding Secrets of the Devil Worshippers' Mystic Love Cult
ROBERT SCHEFFER *Prince Narcissus and Other Stories*
ROBERT SCHEFFER *The Green Fly and Other Stories*
MARCEL SCHWOB *The Assassins and Other Stories*
MARCEL SCHWOB *Double Heart*
COLBY SMITH *The Ironic Skeletons*
SIMEON SOLOMON *Collected Writings*
CHRISTIAN HEINRICH SPIESS *The Dwarf of Westerbourg*
BRIAN STABLEFORD (editor) *The Snuggly Satyricon*
BRIAN STABLEFORD (editor) *The Snuggly Satanicon*
BRIAN STABLEFORD *Spirits of the Vasty Deep*
COUNT ERIC STENBOCK *Love, Sleep and Dreams*

COUNT ERIC STENBOCK *Myrtle, Rue and Cypress*
COUNT ERIC STENBOCK *The Shadow of Death*
COUNT ERIC STENBOCK *Studies of Death*
MONTAGUE SUMMERS *The Bride of Christ and Other Fictions*
MONTAGUE SUMMERS *Six Ghost Stories*
ALICE TÉLOT *The Inn of Tears*
GILBERT-AUGUSTIN THIERRY *The Blonde Tress and The Mask*
GILBERT-AUGUSTIN THIERRY *Reincarnation and Redemption*
GILBERT-AUGUSTIN THIERRY *Stigma and The Pompeiian Fresco*
DOUGLAS THOMPSON *The Fallen West*
FELIX TIMMERMANS *A Peasant Farmer's Psalm*
TOADHOUSE *What Makes the Wave Break?*
LÉO TRÉZENIK *The Confession of a Madman*
LÉO TRÉZENIK *Decadent Prose Pieces*
ANNA JANE VARDILL *The Secrets of Cabalism*
RUGGERO VASARI *Raun*
ROGER VAN DE VELDE *Crackling Skulls*
ILARIE VORONCA *The Confession of a False Soul*
ILARIE VORONCA *The Key to Reality*
JANE DE LA VAUDÈRE *The Demi-Sexes and The Androgynes*
JANE DE LA VAUDÈRE
   The Double Star and Other Occult Fantasies
JANE DE LA VAUDÈRE
   The Mystery of Kama and Brahma's Courtesans
JANE DE LA VAUDÈRE
   Three Flowers and The King of Siam's Amazon
JANE DE LA VAUDÈRE
   The Witch of Ecbatana and The Virgin of Israel
AUGUSTE VILLIERS DE L'ISLE-ADAM *Isis*
RENÉE VIVIEN *Lilith's Legacy*
RENÉE VIVIEN *A Woman Appeared to Me*
RENÉE VIVIEN AND HÉLÈNE DE ZUYLEN DE NYEVELT
   Faustina and Other Stories
ILARIE VORONCA *The Confession of a False Soul*
ILARIE VORONCA *The Key to Reality*
TERESA WILMS MONTT *In the Stillness of Marble*
TERESA WILMS MONTT *Sentimental Doubts*
KAREL VAN DE WOESTIJNE *The Dying Peasant*

www.ingramcontent.com/pod-product-compliance
Lightning Source LLC
Chambersburg PA
CBHW050426110726
47899CB00008B/2870